Coloring book for adults and kids amazing cocking image for design

This coloring book is belongs to

KITCHEN
MILK
I can COOKING!
F

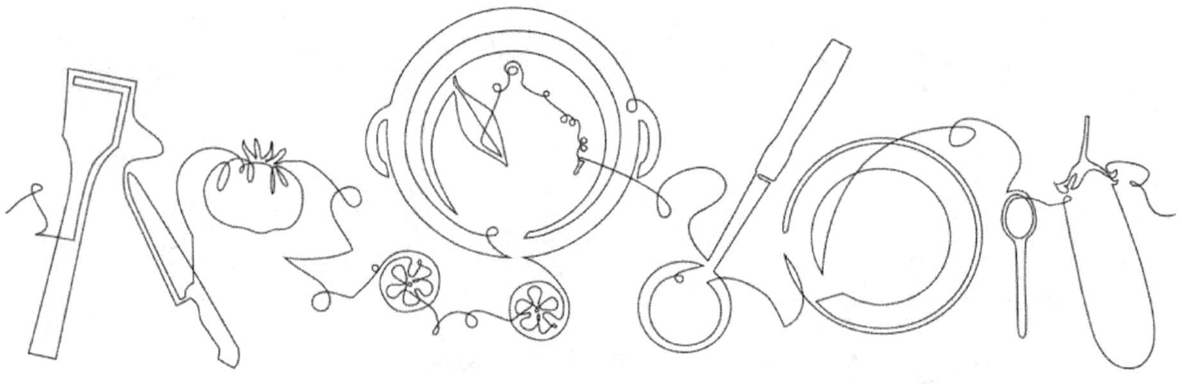

Let's
COOK
together

ReStaurant
CLASSIC RECIPES

LOVE
COOK
ing

COOK
ing

Menu

Cooking
premium

mix taste stir
lemons
1 cup
YEAST
oz.
25 min.
glass
tbs.
ts.
FLOUR
1/2 1/3 1/4 2/3
salted
pound baking unsalted
sugar bake at butter
ADD Pinch of
salt soda

INGREDIENTS
MIX

JUICE

FLOUR
SUGAR
American cuisine
PANCAKE WITH STRAWBERRY AND BANANA

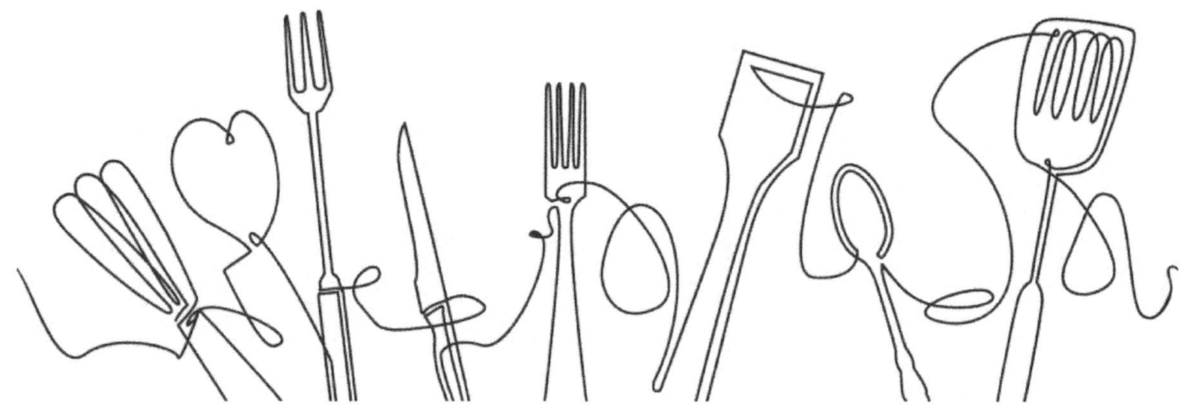

LOUR
SUGAR
American cuisine
PANCAKE WITH STRAWBERRY AND BANANA

cooking equipment
BAKING STUFF
useful things
SUGAR
VANILLA SUGAR
MILK
BAKING SODA

COOKING

MILK
I love
BAKING
VANILLA SUGAR
SUGAR
BAKING SODA

HOW TO COOK PORRIDGE

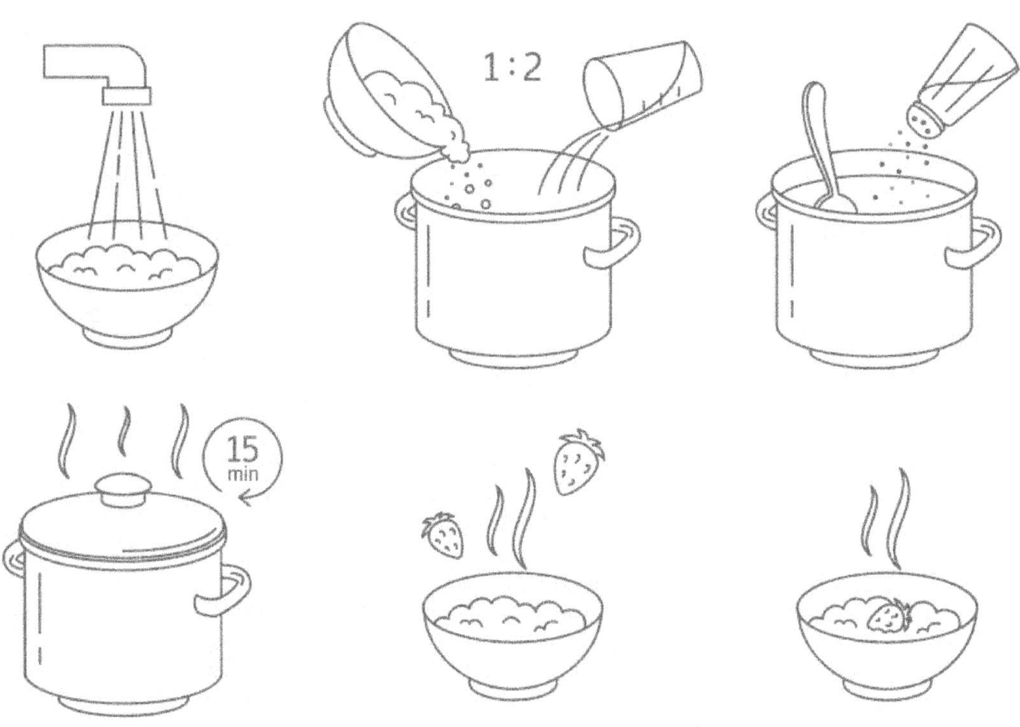

LEMON PIE
FLOUR
EGGS
LEMONS
LEMON ZEST
FLOUR
BUTTER
SUGAR
BAKING SODA
MILK
ADD
MIX
SALT
BAKE
APPLES

Let's
COOK
together

Restaurant
CLASSIC RECIPES

Love
COOK
ing

COOK
ing

Menu

Cooking
premium

LOVE
Cooking.
Recipe

Chocolate Cake

SIMPLE RECIPE

Kitchen

TEA & DESSERT
March
CALENDAR SET
sketch and calligraphy

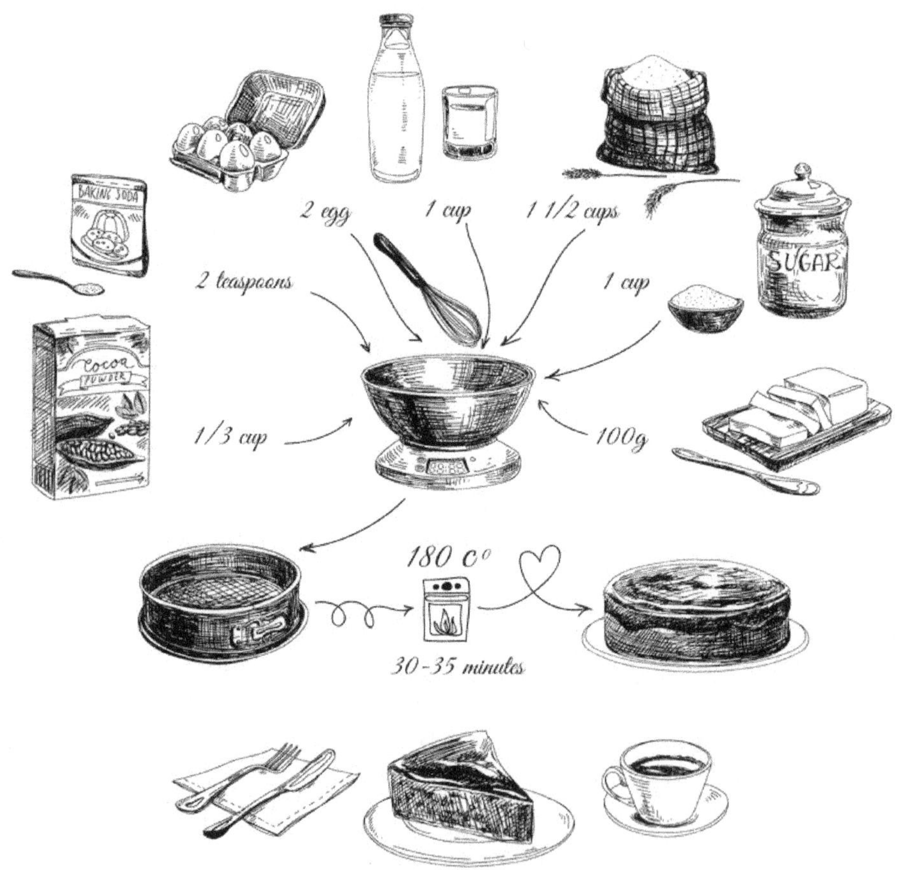
Chocolate Cake
SIMPLE RECIPE
2 egg
1 cup
1 1/2 cups
1 cup
2 teaspoons
SUGAR
2 teaspoons
1/3 cup
100g
BAKING SODA
COCOA POWDER
180 c°
30 - 35 minutes

Lemon Pound Cake
SIMPLE RECIPE

FLOUR
1/2 teaspoon
75g
BAKING SODA
1 teaspoon
For the glaze
200g
2 eggs
1 teaspoon
125ml
200g
SUGAR
100g
1 lemon, juiced
180 c⁰
45 minutes
to 1 hour

pumpkin soup recipe
thyme
onion garlic
carrot pepper cut
cream water
ginger salt mush
seeds

HOW TO MAKE
INSTANT NOODLES

NOODLE SOUP

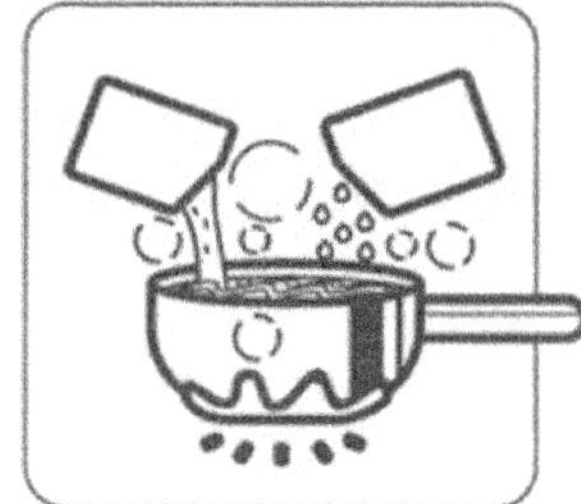

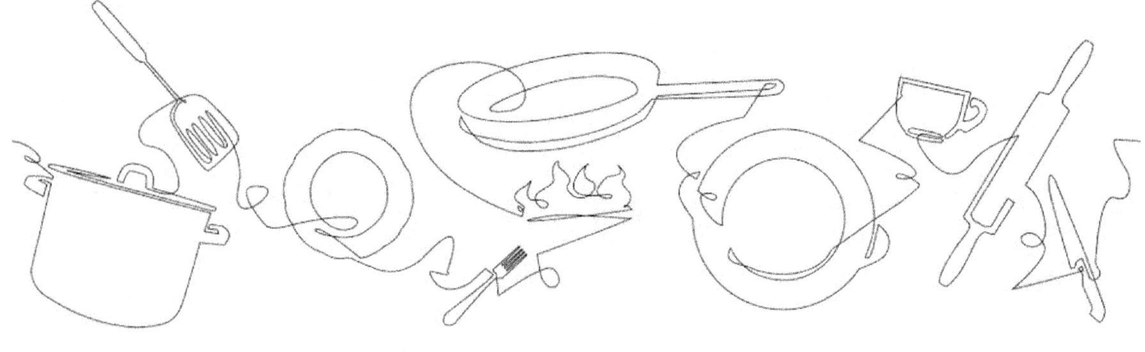

HIGH-TEA

Baked
With
Love

HEALTH
CARE

Fresh Bread

COOKING
Food RECIPE
WHIPPING CREAM
VINEGAR

Doodle Food Set

www.ingramcontent.com/pod-product-compliance
Lightning Source LLC
Chambersburg PA
CBHW081242250726
48654CB00012B/1448